Warrior Women in American History

THE ROLE OF FEMALE CONFEDERATE SPIES IN THE CIVIL WAR

Warrior Women in American History

THE ROLE OF FEMALE CONFEDERATE SPIES IN THE CIVIL WAR

Hallie Murray

Cavendish Square
New York

Published in 2020 by Cavendish Square Publishing, LLC

243 5th Avenue, Suite 136, New York, NY 10016

First Edition

Website: cavendishsq.com

Cataloging-in-Publication Data
Names: Murray, Hallie.
Title: The role of female Confederate spies in the Civil War / Hallie Murray.
Description: New York : Cavendish Square Publishing, 2020. | Series: Warrior women in American history | Includes glossary and index.
Identifiers: ISBN 9781502655400 (pbk.) | ISBN 9781502655417 (library bound) | ISBN 9781502655424 (ebook)
Subjects: LCSH: Women spies–Confederate States of America–Biography–Juvenile literature. | United States–History–Civil War, 1861-1865–Secret service–Biography–Juvenile literature. | United States–History–Civil War, 1861-1865–Participation, Female–Juvenile literature. | United States–History–Civil War, 1861-1865–Biography–Juvenile literature.
Classification: LCC E608.M87 2020 | DDC 973.7'860922 B–dc23

Printed in the United States of America

Portions of this book originally appeared in *Women Civil War Spies of the Confederacy* by Larissa Phillips.

Photo Credits: Cover, p. 3 Everett Collection/Newscom; p. 7 JHU Sheridan Libraries/Gado/Archive Photos/Getty Images; pp. 9, 25, 32-33, 74 Everett Historical/Shutterstock.com; p. 13 Historic Collection/Alamy Stock Photo; pp. 15, 18-19, 29, 43, 44-45, 49, 51, 62, 65 Library of Congress Prints and Photographs Division; pp. 22-23 Universal History Archive/Universal Images Group/Getty Images; p. 35 Art Collection/Alamy Stock Photo; pp. 40-41 Hulton Archive/Getty Images; p. 54 Library of Congress/Corbis Historical/Getty Images; pp. 56-57 Fay 2018/Alamy Stock Photo; pp. 66-67 Matthew Kiernan/Alamy Stock Photo; p. 72 alleged member/Wikimedia Commons/File:Knights of the Golden Circle History of Seccession book, 1862.jpg/Public Domain Mark 1.0; pp. 76-77 Hulton Archive/Archive Photos/Getty Images; p. 80 Chris Light/Wikimedia Commons/File:Virginia 'Ginne' Moon P9120101.jpg/CC BY-SA 4.0; p. 84 Corbis Historical/Getty Images; p. 87 Library of Congress Rare Book and Special Collections Division.

Contents

Introduction

The American Civil War officially began in 1861, when soldiers representing the Confederacy attacked Fort Sumter in Charleston, South Carolina. At the time, the United States was divided between the states that supported the federal government and the Southern states that had seceded from the Union. Some politicians and military leaders defected to the Confederate States of America, the new government in the South. Americans fought bitterly against each other, brother against brother, friend against friend, for four long years, and for a while it looked like the newly formed United States would be ripped apart. When the Confederacy surrendered in 1865, the eleven states that had seceded were folded back into the Union, but not without a massive cost. It was the bloodiest war in America's history, with a staggering death toll, and those who survived faced the monumental task of rebuilding their lives and their nation.

When the war began, supporters of the Confederacy were convinced they would be victorious, as the South seemed to have many advantages over the North. One of these key advantages was geography: because they were fighting to separate from the rest of the United States, the South's objective in the war was merely to stay put and defend its territory. The Union, by contrast, wanted to win

THE BALTIMORE REBEL SONG

1776 VERSUS 1861.

My heart is in the South, boys, my heart is not here,
We will rally round the Red and White, boys, for liberty so dear;
My heart is in the South, boys, and cheerfully I go,
The tyrant host will tremble boys, to meet an honest foe.

My heart is in the South, boys, no iron rule is there
To crush our noble freedom, whose glorious cause we share;
Then rally round the Red and White, boys, our fathers' voices cry,
Our watchword shall be liberty, to conquer or to die.

My heart is in the South, boys, no coward sons are we,
Our fathers shed their blood for us, and should we not be free?
Then rally round the Red and White, boys, and break the oppressors' chain,
For liberty is ours by birth, by many a bloody stain.

My heart is in the South, boys, and echo shall reply,
We'll stand unshaken as the rock for freedom till we die;
Then rally round the Red and White, boys, ne'er wait, or shrink, or pause,
For right shall triumph over might, in this our glorious cause.

My heart is in the South, boys, let us never, never yield,
Our buckler shall be girded tight, and Providence our shield;
Then rally round the Red and White, boys, we glory in ou right,
Though darkness may obscure the day, the morning shall be bright.

This Civil War publication from 1861 offers a battle cry for Confederate supporters living in Baltimore and compares the federal government in 1861 to the tyrannical British government in 1776.

the Southern territory back, meaning Union troops had to travel south, defeat the Southern troops, and occupy its territories in order to achieve success. This demanded a lot more resources than simply staying put and defending the land, as the Southerners had to do. The Confederacy also had an advantage based on lifestyle: because the South had a lot more agriculture and farmland than the North, which had more cities and factories, Southern men were more used to riding horses, firing guns, and living off the land. Northern soldiers, on the other hand, needed to be taught to ride and shoot.

Early on, it seemed like the Confederacy had an advantage when it came to leadership too: military leaders like Robert E. Lee, Stonewall Jackson, and J. E. B. Stuart are remembered as excellent commanders to this day. But while most people have heard about the soldiers and military leaders of the Confederacy, not many know about some of its female participants. Women at the time were not allowed to vote or hold office, but that didn't stop them from holding strong political opinions or acting on them. Many Southern women weren't content to sit at home helplessly while their husbands and brothers and fathers went to war. Instead, they helped the Confederacy in whatever way they could. And one major way women worked to forward the Confederate cause was through spying.

Though not an official component of either side's strategy, both the Union and the Confederacy used espionage to get ahead. Knowledge of the other side's plans and movements could—and often did—make the difference between winning a battle and losing. As the conflict grew, it seemed like everyone involved was spying

Thomas "Stonewall" Jackson was a Confederate general in the Civil War. He earned his nickname during the First Battle of Bull Run, in which a fellow officer said he held back the Union troops like a stone wall.

on everyone else, regardless of their allegiances. Because everyone fighting was American, it was hard to tell whether a person supported the Union or the Confederacy just by looking at them. Civilians from both sides gossiped with each other and with Union and Confederate soldiers, spreading rumors and information in equal measure.

In particular, Washington, DC, became a hotbed of gossip and spying. Although it was a part of the Union, many Southern loyalists either remained in the city or retained their connections to powerful people there. Confederate sympathizers collected information from old acquaintances and new friends alike and delivered key knowledge to their military leaders. Some even chose to remain in Washington specifically in order to continue gathering information.

As Union forces moved South, spying opportunities blossomed in Southern cities and towns. Union officers interacted with local families, occasionally commandeering their homes. The women of these families usually weren't considered a threat in the same way the men were, but perhaps they should have been. Some listened to private discussions through keyholes and doors, while others brazenly pretended at relationships or friendships with Union soldiers in order to gather details that might help the Confederate cause—young women were not above using their looks to fool young soldiers into giving up more information than they should. Before the war, young men and women who now stood on separate sides of the conflict might easily have flirted, danced, or even married. Just because the war was on, this mingling didn't necessarily stop. It just took on a more duplicitous nature.

Because they seemed nonthreatening, women could also sometimes go places soldiers could not, and they could often travel places without attracting suspicion. The Confederacy badly needed things like morphine and other anesthetics to help numb the pain of battlefield amputations, but after the North cut off supply lines to the South, such drugs and other crucial supplies were difficult to get. Soldiers on both sides underestimated women, making it easier for Southern ladies to travel across dangerous territory and smuggle key items from the North to the South.

There were other ways women contributed to the war beyond spying and secrecy. The bloody battlefields dramatically increased the demand for medical help, and many women met that need by serving as nurses. Certain women even disguised themselves as men in order to serve as soldiers. But of all the women who found ways to work for the Confederate cause, the spies are perhaps the least acknowledged. Because of the nature of their work, it's impossible to know just how many female spies there were. Of the few that are known, many go unrecognized, even though their actions likely dramatically affected the outcomes of different battles and campaigns. Regardless of how many there might have been, or who they were, all of them fought hard and performed dangerous deeds because they believed deeply in the cause of the Confederacy. They fought for their beliefs just as hard as any soldier, and though we might not agree with their purpose, it's important to respect their bravery and influence.

1

Wild Rose Greenhow: Washington's High-Society Spy

Many details of Rose O'Neal Greenhow's early life are unknown. She was born sometime between 1813 and 1817 and spent much of her childhood on her father's farm in Montgomery County, Maryland. By 1830, however, both of Rose's parents had passed away, and Rose and her sister Ellen were sent to live with their aunt, who ran a boarding house in Washington, DC, and was well connected among the Washington elite.

High society suited Rose O'Neal. She was beautiful and intelligent, and many men sought to court her. She was considered by at least one contemporary to be "the most persuasive woman ever known in Washington," and "a woman of almost irresistible seductive powers."[1] In 1835, she married forty-three-year-old Dr. Robert Greenhow, an accomplished and wealthy Virginian. Together they had four daughters and enjoyed a prominent social life. They were friends with many rich and powerful people, including former vice president John C. Calhoun, whose

Rose O'Neal Greenhow was born Rose O'Neal in the 1810s. She soon became a fixture of high society in Washington, DC, thanks to the influence of her aunt.

opinions about politics had a significant influence on Rose Greenhow.

War on the Horizon

In 1854, Greenhow's husband died in an accident. Soon after, her eldest daughter married an army officer and moved to Ohio, but Greenhow and her younger three daughters remained in Washington. At the time, tensions were building in the capital, especially around the issue of slavery. The Republican Party of the time wanted to limit the spread of slavery in the territories that would become the American Midwest. Representatives from the South were strongly against this, because slavery was very important to the economies of Southern states that relied on agriculture. They were afraid that if Republicans succeeded in outlawing slavery in the territories, it was only a matter of time until slavery was abolished in the rest of the country.

As the election of 1860 approached, pro-slavery Southern politicians were so scared of what might happen if the Republican candidate were elected that they threatened to secede. When the Republican candidate, Abraham Lincoln, was voted into office, that's exactly what they did: on December 20, 1860, South Carolina announced its intent to secede from the rest of the country.

As the war approached, Greenhow had much to say. She was suspicious of the North's claim to care about slavery. She believed the North merely wanted to destroy the political and economic power of the South and that it was using the slavery issue as a vehicle to do so. She thought that Northerners wanted to drive the black population away and allow their own people to come in

This newspaper sketch from Saturday, March 16, 1861, shows the inaugural procession of President Abraham Lincoln past the gate of the Capitol grounds.

and fill the menial positions of the slave population. She also thought that President Abraham Lincoln had been unfairly elected.

By the time Lincoln was inaugurated on March 4, 1861, seven states had voted to secede. These seven states (South Carolina, Texas, Louisiana, Mississippi, Alabama, Georgia, and Florida) banded together to form the Confederate States of America, also known as the Confederacy. The legislatures of these states believed that slavery was a constitutional right that could not be limited by the federal government.

The Civil War officially began on April 12, 1861, when the Confederacy attacked the military base at Fort Sumter in South Carolina. Lincoln called for volunteers from Southern states to fight for the Union, which angered a number of other state governments. By the end of May 1861, Arkansas, North Carolina, Tennessee, and part of Virginia had also joined the Confederacy.

Greenhow the Spy

When the Civil War began, Washington, DC, was allied with the North. Rose Greenhow was outraged by this. Many people left Washington to join the Confederacy, but Greenhow remained behind, vowing to do everything she could to protect the South that she so loved. She soon began to spy on the Union, using her social connections to obtain information about the Union's strategies. In 1861, she was recruited by Lieutenant Colonel Thomas Jordan, who ran an elaborate espionage ring. Through him, Greenhow learned how to use a cipher to encode her messages and began gathering information from her many powerful acquaintances.

Greenhow became most famous for the influence she had on the First Battle of Bull Run in July 1861. She learned that Union general Irvin McDowell was going to attack Southern troops near Manassas, Virginia. She also discovered how many troops he had and how those troops planned on traveling to Manassas. This was vital information. Greenhow sent a friend into Virginia with this information, dressed as a farm girl. The message, cleverly written in code, was rolled into the woman's hair, which was pinned up. The girl successfully delivered the message to Confederate general P. G. T. Beauregard. Just days later, the First Battle of Bull Run (also called the First Battle of Manassas) was fought. The Union suffered a stunning defeat, at least in part due to Greenhow's work.

Even though many people predicted a short war, the conflict continued to escalate. In Washington, all decorum and civility were falling to pieces. Greenhow wrote the following passage in her diary, "The streets were filled with armed and unarmed ruffians; women were afraid to go singly into the streets for fear of insult; curses and blasphemy rent the air, and no one would have been surprised at any hour at a general massacre of the peaceful inhabitants."[2]

Most women left the city, and Greenhow was urged to do so herself, but she refused: "At whatever peril, I resolved to remain, conscious of the great service I could render my country, my position giving me remarkable facilities for obtaining information."[3] Despite living among enemies during a war, Greenhow refused to be intimidated. One day, she sat in the gallery of the US Senate, observing what she referred to as the "solemn farce of admitting as U.S. senators the bogus members from Western Virginia."[4]

Union and Confederate armies faced off in the First Battle of Bull Run, the first major battle of the Civil War, which took place on July 21, 1861. Intelligence gathered by Rose Greenhow was hugely helpful in bringing about a Confederate victory.

She made a comment regarding her opinion of the proceedings to a friend seated with her. Suddenly a Union officer in front of her turned around and threatened to report Greenhow for treason. She was indignant:

> I leaned forward and said deliberately, "My remarks were addressed to my companions, and not to you; and if I did not discover by your language that you must be ignorant of all the laws of good-breeding, I should take the number of your company and report you to your commanding officer to be punished for your impertinence!"[5]

The Arrest

For a long time, Greenhow continued her spying, often gathering valuable, detailed pieces of information. She knew that she was being followed and observed, but she merely became more cautious. Sometimes she could not resist having fun with the men who were trailing her. She and a friend would turn around suddenly; the person trailing them would turn also, and then Greenhow and her friend would follow him.

But one day she was stopped by two men as she entered her house. Allan Pinkerton, a Chicago detective, had been hired by the Union and had formed the brand-new Secret Service. Increasingly worried about Greenhow's ability to land and convey military intelligence, on August 23, 1861, Pinkerton and his men placed her under arrest. With no warrant, they searched her house and took into custody every friend who came by to visit. Many of these people had just heard that she'd been arrested and had only stopped by to check on her.

Greenhow was outraged. She wrote: "Men rushed with frantic haste into my chamber, into every sanctuary. My beds, drawers, and wardrobes were all upturned; soiled clothes were pounced upon with avidity, and mercilessly exposed; papers that had not seen the light for years were dragged forth."[6] Greenhow was strip-searched by a woman detective and forced to watch as her house was torn apart. Ever cool under fire, she stayed calm and dignified the entire time.

Soon she was trying to figure out how to destroy the many sheets of paper still hidden undisturbed in

Allan Pinkerton

A Scotsman by birth, Allan Pinkerton was born in Glasgow in 1819. He came to the United States in 1842 after secretly marrying a singer named Joan Carfrae. He worked with antislavery activists in Chicago, and his home was used as a stop on the Underground Railroad. After helping arrest a band of counterfeiters, Pinkerton became Chicago's first police detective in 1849. A year later, he formed his own detective agency. When President Lincoln appointed George B. McClellan as the leader of the Union army, McClellan hired Pinkerton to conduct counterintelligence, as Pinkerton's agency had solved a number of train robberies when McClellan worked as vice president of the Illinois Central Railroad. After the Civil War, Pinkerton continued to work as a detective and created a central database for criminal identification records that the FBI still maintains today.

her house that contained information. That night she snuck into the library and took them down from the top shelf. She remembered that her strip search had not necessitated that she remove her stockings, so she had another woman who had been taken into custody conceal the notes in her own stockings. The next day, when the friend was released, the papers were taken to safety. Greenhow remained under house arrest for seven days, while every inch of her home was searched, including the furniture, which was taken apart.

After a week passed, it was announced that her house would be converted into a prison, with other prisoners joining her. With Greenhow in her suite of

Detective Allan Pinkerton, President Abraham Lincoln, and Union general John Alexander McClermand (*from left to right*) pose at a camp during the Battle of Antietam in September 1862.

rooms were a friend named Miss Mackall, Greenhow's daughter Rose, and a servant. (Of Greenhow's three other daughters, one had recently died and two others lived in California.)

Although scrutinized and observed at every turn, Greenhow still managed to continue sending and receiving information. She survived on cheese and crackers, with no exercise and very little sunlight. As the months passed, she grew weak and unhealthy.

Imprisoned in the Capitol

On January 18, 1862, Greenhow and her eight-year-old daughter Rose were moved to the Old Capitol Prison in Washington, DC. Here, conditions were terrible, and Greenhow was treated roughly and with great contempt by the guards. Meanwhile, her celebrity increased. Reporters came to the prison to interview her, and her house was described in detail in all the newspapers, both in the North and South. She later wrote about her prison experiences:

> The tedium of my prison life at this time was greater than I can depict, and I now also began to realise the fact that my physical health was being gradually undermined by want of exercise and want of proper food. A feeling of lassitude was stealing over me, and a nervous excitability which prevented me from sleeping. My child's health was failing alarmingly also. I had nothing to read, and even the newspapers were served or not, according to the caprice of my jailors, and were very sure to be withheld whenever they contained Southern news. My room swarmed

Rose Greenhow poses with her daughter "Little Rose." Little Rose helped her mother share information with other Confederate spies and lived in the Old Capitol Prison during Greenhow's imprisonment.

> with vermin, which the warm weather now caused to come out in myriads from their hiding-places; and, although at this time allowed the half-hour exercise in the prison yard, I could not regard it as relaxation.[7]

In April 1862, Greenhow had a trial in which she nearly took control of the courtroom, accusing the court of treason. Some time after this, she was released and deported to Richmond, Virginia, where she was greeted by cheering crowds.

Death at Sea

That summer, Confederate president Jefferson Davis sent Greenhow to Europe as a courier. She gathered diplomatic information for him, wrote her memoirs, and publicized the plight of the South. As in Washington, she enjoyed a brilliant social career in Europe, being received in the royal courts of both England and France. In 1864, she returned to the United States.

With important dispatches to deliver, Greenhow boarded the *Condor*, a British blockade-runner. In addition to her bag of mail, she had $3,000 worth of gold coins in a satchel, which was sewn into her clothing. It was not a smooth journey. At the mouth of Cape Fear River outside of Wilmington, North Carolina, a Union ship pursued the *Condor*. In its effort to escape, the *Condor* was forced aground on a sandbar on October 1.

Determined not to be imprisoned again, Greenhow and two others boarded a lifeboat and tried to make it to the shore on their own. But they could not navigate the stormy seas. The lifeboat overturned. Greenhow might have been able to swim to shore were it not for the gold sewn into her dress. There was no hope of surviving with such weight pulling her down. The famous spy met her death in the Atlantic Ocean before the war had even ended. Her body was found a few days later. In a coffin wrapped with a Confederate flag, she was later buried with military honors in the Oakdale Cemetery in Wilmington, North Carolina. Her epitaph, which is inscribed in marble below a cross that bears her name, reads that she was a bearer of messages to the Confederate government.

2

Belle Boyd: The Siren of the Shenandoah

Maria Isabella "Belle" Boyd was born in 1844 in what is now West Virginia to a wealthy Southern family. She eventually became one of the most daring and well-known spies of the Civil War. Though not remembered as particularly beautiful, Boyd captured the hearts and minds of men on both sides of the conflict with her vivaciousness and bold confidence. She used her connections and flirtatious demeanor to ferret out information and complete dangerous missions on behalf of the Confederacy, gaining a long list of cheeky nicknames in the process, including the "Siren of the Shenandoah" and "Cleopatra of the Secession."

Boyd grew up in Martinsburg, Virginia, the eldest child of Benjamin Reed Boyd and Mary Rebecca Glenn Boyd. She had a relatively easy childhood and was adored and indulged by her parents. "I passed my childhood as all happy children usually do," she later wrote, "petted and caressed by a father and mother ... and beloved by brothers and sister."[1] She was athletic, outspoken, and passionate.

Belle Boyd became one of the most famous Confederate spies during the the Civil War. She had many nicknames, including “Cleopatra of the Secession” and “Rebel Joan of Arc.”

Once, when Boyd was eleven, she was barred from attending one of her parents' dinner parties because she was too young. In response, she surprised her parents and their guests by riding into the middle of the dining room on her horse. Though Boyd was not old enough to join in the festivities, she claimed her horse was.

The following year, Boyd was sent to Mount Washington, a girls' finishing school outside of Baltimore. She excelled in her studies and remained outspoken and energetic. Since Maryland was on the border between the North and the South, students at the school held mixed but impassioned views on the coming war. Naturally, Boyd was a vocal participant in the debates between students over which side was right. She defended the South and the institution of slavery, which she believed was an imperfect but necessary part of society. She would continue to defend the South throughout the war through espionage and other covert activities.

War Comes to Washington

At age sixteen, Boyd graduated from Mount Washington. She spent the winter of 1860 to 1861 in Washington, DC, chaperoned by her mother and her slave, Eliza. A true social butterfly, Boyd thrived as a debutante, going to parties, the theater, and political events. She also acquired a collection of suitors who were smitten with her lively personality. That winter, "for the last time for many years to come," she later wrote, "the daughters of the North and the South commingled in sisterly love and friendship."[2]

The good times were about to end. Abraham Lincoln had just been elected president, and the tensions between the North and the South increased. That same winter, seven states—Alabama, Florida, Georgia, Louisiana, Mississippi, South Carolina, and Texas—seceded from the Union and set up a new nation: the Confederate States of America. Virginia seceded from the Union later, on April 17, 1861. Robert E. Lee, a US Army officer, resigned from the US Army to command the Army of Northern Virginia. Boyd's father enlisted.

Boyd herself returned to Martinsburg and joined the war effort with passion and dedication. Beyond raising money and acting as a nurse, she shocked her friends by walking the streets alone and frequently waved to both

Female Nurses in the Civil War

British nurse Florence Nightingale is credited with popularizing the nursing profession for women. She became famous for her work on the battlefield during the Crimean War, and in 1860, she established the first nonreligious nursing school in the world at St. Thomas' Hospital in London. In the early 1860s, however, nursing was still considered unseemly for middle- and upper-class women in America because of the taboos against women working. But the Civil War created a massive demand for medical support, which was eagerly filled by the women on both sides who wanted to help the war efforts. Recognizing the desperate need for qualified nurses, the Confederate Congress passed legislation in 1862 that allowed for the formal enlistment of female hospital workers. Thus, the Civil War provided the first careers for many women and helped to change their earlier roles in society as homemakers.

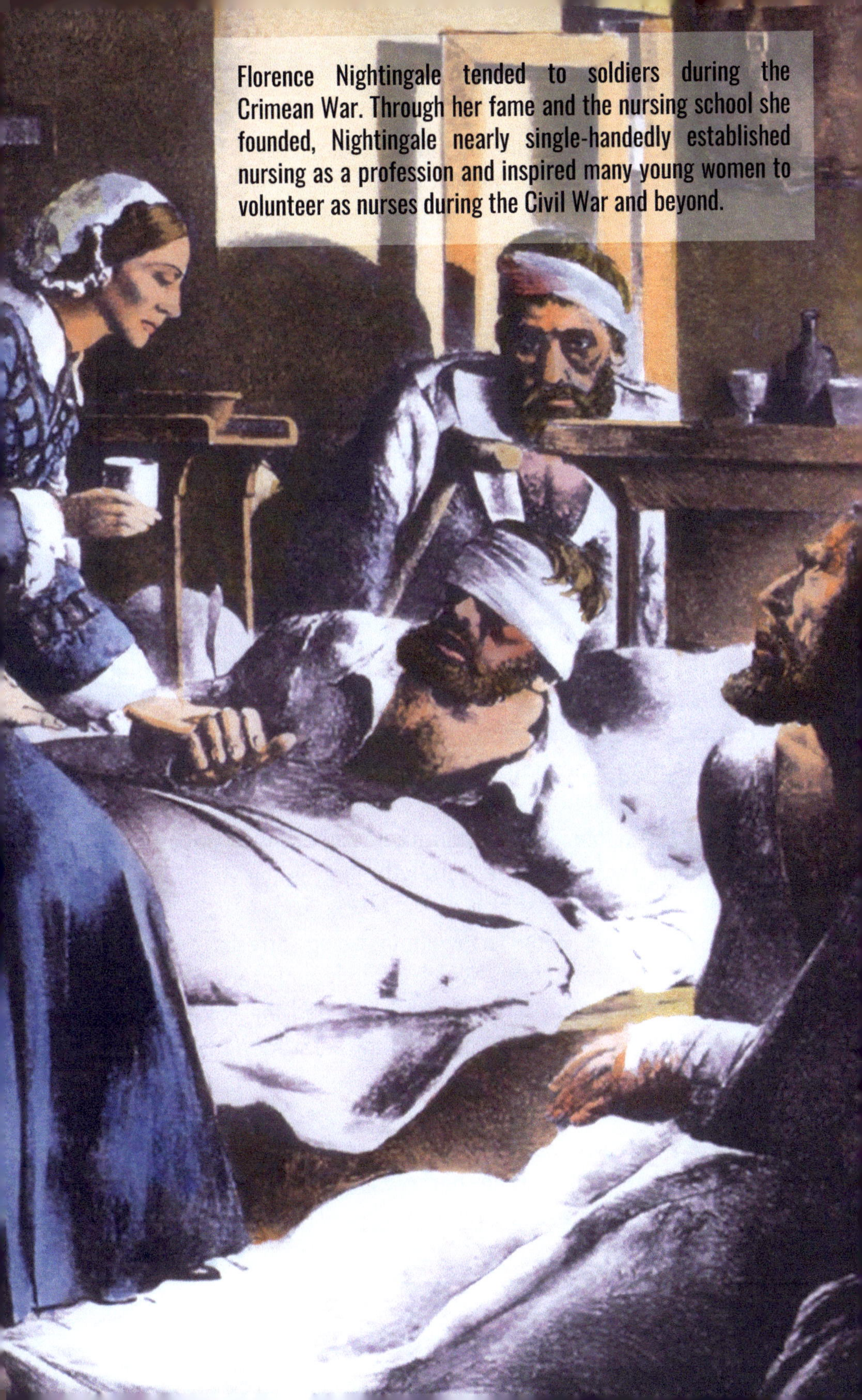

Florence Nightingale tended to soldiers during the Crimean War. Through her fame and the nursing school she founded, Nightingale nearly single-handedly established nursing as a profession and inspired many young women to volunteer as nurses during the Civil War and beyond.

Confederate and Union soldiers. Later, she would visit the military camps and even organize dances with soldiers. But outrageous as this behavior was, her notoriety had hardly begun.

Shooting to Kill

Loyal to the Southern cause, Boyd's mother, Mary, kept a Confederate flag hung outside the Boyd house. On July 4, 1861, a group of Union soldiers came to the Boyd house to take it down. By the time they arrived, Mary had hidden the flag. Unsatisfied, the drunken soldiers began instead trying to raise a Union flag in front of the Boyd house. Boyd's normally reserved mother was furious. "Men," she said to the rowdy group that had taken over her house, "every member of my household will die before that [Union] flag shall be raised over us."[3] The soldiers cursed her. At this, Boyd stepped forward with her arm raised, a gun in hand. Before anyone knew what was happening, she had shot and, by some accounts, killed one of the Union soldiers. "I could stand it no longer," she later wrote. "My indignation was aroused beyond my control. My blood was literally boiling in my veins. I drew out my pistol and shot him."[4]

Boyd was acquitted without being arrested, but her house was put under watch. Totally unfazed, she used the opportunity to flirt with and befriend the soldiers who were supposed to be monitoring her. Soon, Boyd was pulling information from them. She sent Eliza to deliver the messages to the troops.

As a writer, Boyd was bold but not clever. She wrote the notes longhand, in her own writing. Since it didn't occur to her to use a cipher (a symbolic code), one of her

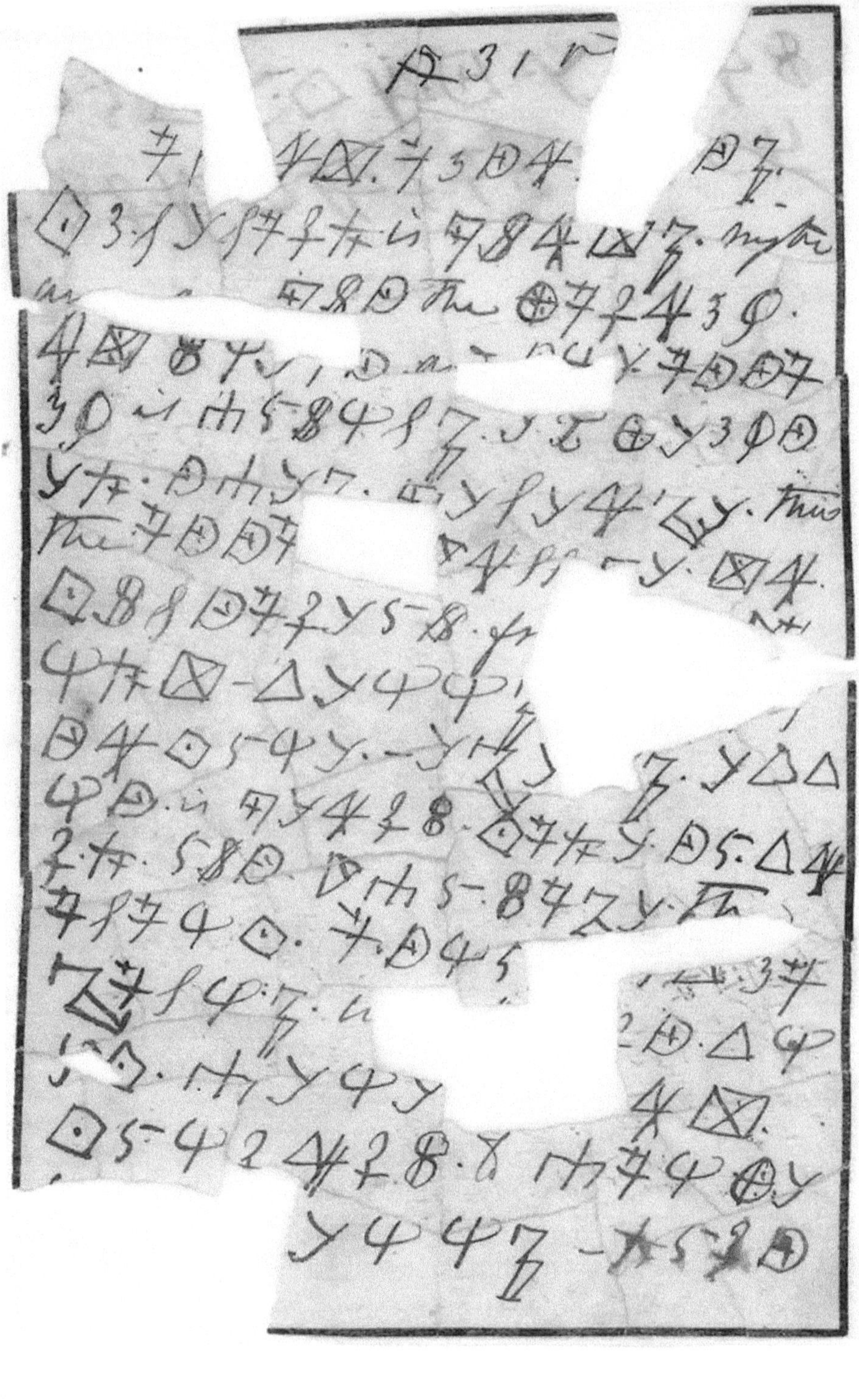

This letter, written by Confederate spy Rose Greenhow, offers an example of a cipher used by Southern spies to communicate secret information to each other and to military personnel.

messages was soon intercepted by the Union army. Boyd was taken into federal headquarters, but because of her age and gender, she was released with a mere warning. Unpunished, she left the federal headquarters more committed than ever to serving the Confederate war effort.

The Battle of Front Royal

Soon the war escalated. Boyd's parents sent her to stay with her aunt and uncle in Front Royal, Virginia. Little did they know that the real action was about to unfold in this town south of Martinsburg. Boyd used her aunt and uncle's hotel, which had been taken over by Union general James Shields, as a base for her espionage exploits. One spring evening in 1862, a Union council was being held in the dining room. Boyd eavesdropped from above, lying in a closet with her ear pressed to a knothole that she had enlarged. When the meeting ended, she rode 14 miles (22.5 kilometers) to tell Confederate general Turner Ashby what had been said and was home before dawn.

Another evening, Boyd sat by the window reading to her grandmother and her cousin, not knowing that one of the greatest nights of her life was about to happen. Suddenly, one of the servants entered in near hysterics, shouting that the rebels were coming to town. Boyd dashed down to the street. There was chaos and confusion everywhere. Union soldiers were running in every direction. She stopped one of them and with the greatest sincerity begged to know what was happening. Unwittingly, he told her that the Confederate generals Stonewall Jackson and Richard Ewell were bringing their troops to town. He bragged to Boyd that the Union army had already captured some of the Confederate troops. The soldier explained the Union's battle plans and its intention to destroy the bridges and close the roads as the troops left town. Essentially, the Confederate soldiers were marching straight into a trap.

Boyd later wrote, "I was in possession of much important information, which, if I could only contrive to convey to General Jackson, I knew our victory would be secure. Without it I had every reason to anticipate defeat and disaster."[5] She quickly tied on a white bonnet and dashed outside. There were soldiers and civilians everywhere in the streets. She pushed through the throngs as fast as she could, dodging and darting, trying not to choke on the dust. She had 10 miles (16 km) to run and many obstacles in her path. But she was hardly dressed for a day of bullet-dodging: "I had on a dark-blue dress, with a little fancy white apron over it; and this contrast of colors, being visible at a great distance, made me far more conspicuous than was just then agreeable."[6]

As Boyd ran, some Union soldiers fired at her. The rifles blazed, some of the bullets hitting the ground around her, causing dust to get into her eyes. Other bullets singed her dress. She later wrote that it was miracle she survived. Still, she kept running. At one point, a shell burst upon the ground not 20 feet (6 meters) from her. She had just enough time to throw herself onto the ground, where she waited out the explosion.

"I shall never run again as I ran on that, to me, memorable day," she wrote. "Hope, fear, the love of life, and the determination to serve my country to the last, conspired to fill my heart with more than feminine courage, and to lend preternatural strength and swiftness to my limbs."[7]

With her chest heaving, her muscles shaking, and her dress burnt and ragged from rifle fire, Boyd made it to the first of the Confederate troops. She saw an officer she recognized, Major Harry Douglas. As he held her hand, incredulous at the sight of this woman on the battlefield, she caught her breath and then delivered the message for which she had risked her life. Douglas galloped off to find General Jackson, and Boyd was free to go. Her mission was completed.

The Confederates successfully defended the bridges, and Boyd's name became widely known. Just days later, Stonewall Jackson wrote to her: "I thank you, for myself and for the Army, for the immense service that you have rendered your country."[8]

Prison Life

After her stunning delivery at Front Royal, Boyd continued to act as a spy, carrying messages and letters to Richmond. But she was not as careful as she could have been. By now she was famous—the daring young rebel spy had been written about in newspapers throughout the North and South. On July 29, 1862, she was arrested by a US Secret Service detective. He escorted her to Washington, DC, and put her in the Old Capitol Prison.

Prison life was tolerable for Boyd. She was allowed to keep her own trunk of belongings and was told by the superintendent that so long as she remained in her own cell and did not communicate with the other prisoners, her door would remain unlocked. She was offered the use of a servant and given a choice of meals—often supplemented with sweets from admirers outside the prison walls. Still, there were decayed walls, bedding infested with lice and bedbugs, and a chill to the room.

On her first night in prison, the superintendent ushered in the detective chief, Lafayette C. Baker, who attempted to get a confession from Boyd. When he could not, he urged her to give an oath of allegiance to the Union. Boyd was offended. She firmly declared her refusal: "I would rather lie down in this prison and die, than leave it owing allegiance to such a government as yours. Now leave the room; for so thoroughly am I disgusted with your conduct towards me, that I cannot endure your presence longer."[9]

No sooner had she finished this tongue-lashing than the other prisoners on her floor erupted in cheers and shouts. She hadn't realized that her door was open and her speech was audible to all. Even the tough superintendent was taken with her charming fearlessness.

Espionage Across the Confederacy

Boyd spent scarcely a month in prison before she was released and allowed to return to Virginia. Once home, she wasted no time in resuming her espionage activities and capitalizing on her fame. The day after she arrived home, she rode out to the encampment where General Jackson could be found. Here, she received a welcome that made all the danger she'd faced seem worthwhile. "As I dismounted at the door of his tent," she later wrote, "he came out, and, gently placing his hands upon my head, assured me of the pleasure he felt at seeing me once more well and free. Our interview was of necessity short, for the demands upon his valuable time were incessant; but his fervent 'God bless you, my child,' will never be obliterated

The Old Capitol Prison got its name because Congress met there after the Capitol was burned in the War of 1812. During the Civil War, it housed Confederate prisoners like Rose Greenhow and Belle Boyd.

from my memory, as long as Providence shall be pleased to allow it to retain its power."[10]

Around this time, there was word of President Lincoln's Emancipation Proclamation, which called for the end of slavery in the Confederacy. This declaration added fuel to the intensity of the war. On General Jackson's advice, Boyd moved to Winchester and there received a commission as captain and honorary aide-de-camp to Jackson. She wrote, "Thenceforth I enjoyed the respect paid to an officer by soldiers."[11] After some months of enjoying this, the Union soldiers approached, and Boyd restlessly moved about the South before returning home.

But Martinsburg was soon placed under federal occupation, and Boyd was arrested. Later, she was summoned to Washington and put into Carroll Prison. As an inmate, she made friends with the other women, flirted with the guards, and sang Southern songs in an impassioned voice for all to hear. One night she was surprised when an arrow flew through the window and landed on the opposite wall. A letter was attached, expressing sympathy and friendship. It gave Boyd instructions for how to correspond secretly with "C.H.," the writer of the letter. In this manner, she was able to communicate with the outside world and exasperate the guards. They knew she was in communication with someone, but they could never catch her in the act.

Spy No More

Eventually, prison life wore Boyd down, and she contracted typhoid fever. After many weeks, she recovered—just in time to be sentenced to hard labor at the Fitchburg, Massachusetts, jail for the rest of the war. Thanks to

The Emancipation Proclamation was an executive order issued by President Lincoln on January 1, 1863, that legally freed all slaves in the South, though it was difficult to enforce in practice.

NO PARKING
E. RACE

The Belle Boyd House in Martinsburg, West Virginia, is a museum and landmark that preserved the original home of Belle Boyd's family.

her father's influence, her sentence was reduced to banishment from the North for the duration of the war. This was more of a hardship than it might seem: since Virginia had split into Virginia and West Virginia, Boyd's hometown of Martinsburg was now in the North. She wouldn't ever be able to go home.

On December 1, 1863, she was released from Carroll Prison and sent to Richmond. No sooner had she arrived in the city than she learned her father had died. Although she appealed to many powerful figures, Boyd was unable to receive permission to visit Martinsburg to pay her last respects to her father.

Distraught and discouraged, Boyd had the idea of going to Europe, where she could act as a courier for the Confederate cause. On the way, she met a federal officer, Sam Hardinge. Their shipboard romance soon escalated, and the two were married in England. However, Hardinge returned to the United States almost immediately and died on his way back to London, perhaps on a sunken ship. The details of his death are unclear.

Alone in England and expecting a child, Boyd decided to write about her experiences to support herself. In May 1865, *Belle Boyd, in Camp and Prison* was published in London. It was well received and was soon published in the United States. The following year, she turned to the stage, playing the lead female role in a small play. That was also the year her daughter Grace was born and the year that President Andrew Johnson issued a Proclamation of Amnesty, which allowed her to return home.

She continued her theatrical career until the age of twenty-five. At that time, she married a successful businessman named John Swainston Hammond. The newlyweds moved to California and had three more children. Boyd divorced Hammond in 1884, and at forty-one years of age, she remarried yet again. As her new husband was an actor, his income was insufficient to support Boyd, and she returned to the stage. This time she recited monologues about her exploits as a spy.

In June 1900, Belle Boyd suffered a heart attack and died. She was fifty-six years old. To say that she had lived life to the fullest and pushed the limits of what society expected of a woman would hardly be an exaggeration.

3

Antonia Ford: Stuart's Southern Lady

Born in 1838 in Fairfax Court House, Virginia, Antonia Ford was a privileged young woman whose work for the Confederacy centered around her family home in Fairfax Court House. Ford grew up in a wealthy family and attended the Buckingham Female Collegiate Institute for finishing school in 1857. Known for her beauty and her good manners, Ford seemed every bit the charming debutante, a perception she used to her advantage when it came to gathering information. One historian says that Ford "spent no small part of her time in primping before a large looking-glass in her room trying on one dress after another, arranging her beautiful dark blond hair and posing with her gorgeously colored fan. She is said to have cultivated a voice so sweet and subdued as to add to her seductive appeal."[1]

Spying for General Stuart

Although the Ford family lived in Northern Virginia, they were firmly in support of the Confederacy. In fact, Ford's brother was a member of the artillery company of Confederate general J. E. B. "Jeb" Stuart, and Ford

This sketch, titled *General Stuart's New Aid*, shows Antonia Ford on horseback. The original caption noted that Ford "has been of great service to [Jeb Stuart] in giving information."

soon found herself sitting down to dinner with Stuart and his scout, a dangerous Confederate private named John Singleton Mosby. Because Stuart's cavalry was posted near the Ford home in Fairfax, Stuart and Mosby were frequent guests there during the early part of the war. Stuart was soon fond of this young woman. Not only was she a delightful dining companion, but she was also a passionate supporter.

In June 1861, the Army of the Potomac left Washington, DC, and headed for what would become the First Battle of Bull Run. On its way, the army went through Fairfax Courthouse. A fevered skirmish led to the death of John Quincy Marr, the first Confederate officer to die in battle. After the brief fight, Ford watched as her beloved Southern troops left Fairfax and Union troops took over. The Union soldiers moved into the Ford home and used it as a boardinghouse, just as their Confederate counterparts had done. It was there that Ford began her career as a spy. Using her charm on the Union soldiers staying in her family's home, she carefully pulled information from them and gave those facts to Stuart.

One day, the Yankee officers ordered a search of the local houses. Ford caught wind of the inspection in time to make some preparations. When the soldiers arrived, they found her sitting in her parlor, looking harmless, with her skirts arranged artfully about her. She read and fanned herself as the soldiers searched the room. When they were almost finished, an officer asked her to stand. Ford acted as offended as if he had slapped her. "I thought not even a Yankee would expect a Southern woman to rise for him,"[2] she said. The soldier backed down sheepishly, leaving important documents safely hidden under Ford's skirts.

Confederate general J. E. B. Stuart had a reputation for being well-dressed and coiffed, though he was also known as a serious leader.

General Jeb Stuart

James Ewell Brown Stuart, known as Jeb for his initials, was born on a plantation in Virginia to a family of slaveholders. He graduated from West Point in 1854 and was assigned to a unit in Texas. Stuart was a skilled cavalryman and cut a dashing figure, as he often wore a colorful cap and sash with a plumed hat. In 1861, he was promoted to captain, but he resigned from the US Army less than two weeks after this appointment to join the Confederate army after Virginia seceded. He helped the Confederacy win a number of battles, but his mistakes at the Battle of Gettysburg were generally believed to have contributed to Lee's defeat there. He died on May 12, 1864, after being struck by a bullet at the Battle of Yellow Tavern.

In October 1861, Stuart presented Ford with a document that named her an honorary member of his staff. One witness later said that while the document was official in nature, the presentation was playful and somewhat in jest.[3] Just twenty-eight years of age when the war began, Stuart was known for his brilliant leadership as well as for his flamboyant style. It is easy to imagine him presenting a woman with a mock certificate. Regardless of the intention, this commission would eventually have far-reaching effects on Ford's career as a spy.

The Capture of Edwin Stoughton

Right before the Second Battle of Bull Run in August 1862, Ford saved Southern troops from certain defeat by eavesdropping on Union officers. She learned beforehand that they planned to use Confederate colors to draw the Confederate soldiers away from their assigned positions. When she could find no one to deliver the message about the Union's plan for her, she set out to deliver it herself. Ford climbed into a carriage alone and drove 20 miles (32 km) through the rain and directly past Union troops to deliver the information to Stuart.

But her greatest coup was yet to come. When the Union general Edwin Stoughton set up headquarters at Fairfax Courthouse and began gathering troops there, Ford informed Stuart and Mosby of the Union troops' movements. Stuart and Mosby were busy bombarding Stoughton's men with sudden attacks and sneak raids followed by stealthy withdrawals. It is likely that Ford helped them to avoid being captured, as Stuart and Mosby informed their troops not be lured away from their original positions.

At the same time, Ford was on friendly terms with Stoughton, going for rides in the country with him and causing much speculation and gossip among his men. Once, she and Stoughton met Mosby in the forest. Since Stoughton did not know it was Mosby, Ford calmly introduced him as a local friend of hers. On another occasion, it was said that she had entertained Mosby in her home.

On March 8, 1863, Stoughton, who was just twenty-four years old and had a reputation as a womanizer and a drinker, hosted a party at a local home in Fairfax. Because of the party, Union security was lax, and because there was rain that night, outdoor noises were muffled. It was a perfect night for a Mosby-style raid. After assembling in the forest, Mosby and his men descended upon the town.

Brigadier General Edwin H. Stoughton, shown here, is most famous for being captured while asleep by John S. Mosby, the Confederate commander nicknamed the "Gray Ghost."

Telegraph wires were cut. Prized horses were stolen. Union officers were taken prisoner.

Later that night, Mosby himself stole into Stoughton's bedroom. The general was asleep, with empty champagne bottles strewn about his room. According to some accounts, Mosby lifted the general's nightshirt and smacked him on the rear. "Did you ever hear of Mosby?" he asked the sputtering young general. Stoughton sat up in bed and exclaimed, "Yes! You've caught him?" Mosby grinned in the dark. "He's caught you!"[4] Stoughton's capture led to his arrest and imprisonment and was a humiliating blow to the Union troops.

Ford's Arrest

Union officers were incensed by Stoughton's capture. Under great pressure to lay blame, the US Secret Service chief, Lafayette Baker, immediately suspected espionage. He wrote the following in a report about the incident.

> The time, circumstances, and mode of this attack and surprise, the positive and accurate knowledge in possession of the rebel leader, of the numbers and position of our forces, of the exact localities of officers' quarters, and depots of Government property, all pointed unmistakably to the existence of traitors and spies within our lines.[5]

Although Mosby insisted that Ford had not given him information, she remained a primary suspect, so Baker and his men devised a plan to catch her. A female Union spy, Frankie Abel, posed as a refugee from New Orleans. Abel showed up in Fairfax in ragged clothes and easily deceived the townspeople, including Ford and her family.

Antonia Ford is buried in the Oak Hill Cemetery in Washington, DC, which also holds the bodies of figures like Edwin Stanton—Lincoln's secretary of war—and Chief Justice Edward Douglass White.

The Fords took Abel in, dressed her in fine clothing, and made her comfortable in their home. She formed a friendship with Ford, and they traded stories about their exploits in service to the Confederacy. At one point, Ford showed off her commission from General Stuart.

This was the hard evidence linking Ford to treasonable activity. On May 3, 1863, a few days after Abel left, Ford and her father were placed under arrest. Ford's father was let go quickly, but Ford remained in prison until May 20, when she was released in a prisoner exchange. It was only shortly after that, though, that she was arrested again and taken to the Old Capitol Prison in Washington, D.C.

Marriage and the End

While in prison, she enjoyed one great advantage over the other prisoners: the swooning attention of a handsome Union officer, Major Joseph C. Willard. Back in Fairfax, where Willard had been the provost marshal, he had been an admirer of Ford's. When she was placed under arrest, by chance he was assigned to escort her to prison. He then began campaigning for her release. Willard was successful, and Ford was released in September 1863. Seven months later, on March 10, 1864, they married.

Ford later wrote to Willard of their first meeting, "I think fate has a good deal to do with us ... It seems I was literally thrown in your way by a power above us—call it Destiny."[6] They had three children, two of whom died in infancy. After seven years, Ford died and was buried in Oak Hill Cemetery in Washington, DC. Some believed that her early death was caused by her harsh confinement in the Old Capitol Prison, after which she had never regained her health; others say it was a consequence of childbearing.

Her husband never remarried. Ford's career as a spy was somewhat short-lived, but she was indispensable in one of the more embarrassing events for the Union—the capture of Edwin Stoughton.

4

Charlotte Moon: The Costumed Messenger

Charlotte "Lottie" Moon and Virginia "Ginnie" Moon were sisters who both worked to further the Confederate cause through espionage and other secret activities. Though fifteen years apart, the Moon sisters were both known for their vibrant, assertive personalities and their acting skills. They were bold flirts who seemed to enjoy committing acts of outrageous daring, from carrying messages to fooling Union officials with various accents and disguises to smuggling medical supplies under their hoop skirts.

Lottie, the older of the two, was born in Virginia in 1828, though the family eventually moved to Oxford, Ohio, after Ginnie was born in 1844. Although they were raised in Ohio, the sisters remained Southerners in their hearts for years to come. Their father, Robert Moon, was from an old Virginia family. He was a gentle, scholarly man who worked as a physician. Their mother was a rigid Orthodox Presbyterian. Although their parents were respectable citizens, the children were raised unconventionally. The girls read biographies, science, and even Charles Darwin, works that were then considered highly controversial.

As a teenager, Lottie practiced shooting with a gun, rode a horse bareback (without a saddle) through town, and nursed fantasies of becoming an actress. She was headstrong and willful. For a time, she was engaged to future Union general Ambrose Burnside, but according to legend, she left him at the altar after answering "No sirree Bob!" when the minister asked if she would take him as her husband.[1] After leaving Burnside at the altar, she married Jim Clark, a suitor much closer to her own age. Clark was an attorney who later became a judge. There are rumors that even at this wedding, a second suitor showed up at the church thinking it might be his lucky day.

An Actress Turned Spy

When the war started, the entire family rooted fervently for the South. Lottie and Ginnie's two brothers joined the Confederate army. When Robert Moon died, the widowed Mrs. Moon sent Ginnie to Oxford Female College in Ohio, and she herself moved back to Memphis. Lottie and her husband remained in Ohio and became active members of the Knights of the Golden Circle, a secret society with Confederate sympathies. Undercover couriers frequently stopped at the Clark household.

In 1862, a man named Walker Taylor knocked on the Clarks' door. He was traveling from Kentucky under a false name, supposedly to sell mules. In reality, he was an undercover courier, with vital messages to deliver to General Edmund Kirby-Smith in Kentucky. But he was too well known to make the trip into occupied territory, where Union soldiers would be keeping a careful eye on civilian travelers.

Edmund Kirby-Smith was the general in charge of the Trans-Mississippi Department, the region of the Confederacy that covered most of the area west of the Mississippi River.

Lottie immediately volunteered to make the delivery. She dressed up as a toothless old woman, giving herself a hunchback and wearing a bonnet and a ragged shawl. Convincingly disguised, she crossed the Ohio River by ferry. On the other side, she found a Union transport preparing to leave for Lexington, Kentucky—her destination. A less daring person might have tried to avoid contact with Union soldiers. But Lottie jumped at the chance for a more direct route and perhaps the chance to prove her mettle.

Adopting an Irish accent, she told the soldiers she was trying to visit her sick husband in Lexington and begged them to give her a ride. At first they said no. But Lottie continued begging, crying, and carrying on, even appealing to soldiers who she thought might be Irish. Finally, the soldiers agreed and smuggled her aboard.

Once in Lexington, she happened to run into a Southerner she'd once met, a colonel for the Confederate army. Straightening up, she thrust the papers into his hand and made him swear he would deliver them to General Kirby-Smith.

With her mission accomplished, she headed back to Ohio on the train, again disguised as the old woman. It was a lucky thing she kept her disguise; once aboard, she overheard that there was a watch out for a female spy. Instead of trying to avoid attention, she promptly began wailing, until a Union general seated near her named Combs turned his head and tried to quiet her. This time, her story grew to include hungry children, an ailing husband, and a fear that she would be mistaken for a spy. General Combs comforted her and promised he would watch out for her safety. When the train arrived in Covington, Kentucky, the general himself gallantly helped this "poor old lady" down from the train. From there she took the ferry home.

Charlotte the Courier

After such a stunning debut, Lottie naturally continued transporting messages. Her next big assignment took her to Toronto, Canada, where she picked up documents that needed to be delivered to Virginia. To get there, Lottie pretended she was a British woman and in poor health. She claimed that she was on her way to Virginia's hot springs. With forged papers, she talked her way into obtaining a traveler's pass to Virginia with an inspired story.

Ambrose Burnside

Born in 1824 in Indiana, Ambrose Burnside began his military career serving throughout the Western frontier. In 1852, he was assigned to Rhode Island, where he married Mary Richmond Bishop. Burnside was serving as a colonel in the Rhode Island Militia when the Civil War began, and he was soon appointed major general of volunteers for his efforts on behalf of the Union in Virginia, particularly at the First Battle of Bull Run and the Battles of Roanoke Island and New Bern. Unfortunately, he faced challenges and made poor decisions while in command at both the Battle of Antietam and the Battle of Fredericksburg, and he was eventually removed from command. After the war, he served as governor of Rhode Island for three years and held a number of other military and political postings before passing away at the age of fifty-seven.

Ambrose Burnside was a general in the Union Army who later became a politician in Rhode Island. His magnificent facial hair inspired the name for "sideburns."

The Moon family's Ohio home is now known as the Lottie Moon House and is part of the campus of Miami University in Ohio.

She said she had crossed the ocean to seek out these curative springs and couldn't die without first trying them.

Pass in hand, Lottie made it to Virginia, delivered the papers, and collected new documents to bring back to Toronto. But she ran into trouble on her way home. Having not actually made it to the thermal springs, she was not well informed on their location. When questioned further, she goofed. Now exposed as a potential fraud, Lottie found herself at the mercy of Union officers. The general interrogating her became suspicious and demanded a surgeon's opinion. Lottie cried and faked her way through the exam, convincing the surgeon that she had severe rheumatism. At the end of the exam, she was taken to her carriage and given another pass.

Burned by Burnside

Lottie's courier activities provided a great outlet for her dramatic personality. She continued acting as a courier until she stumbled upon a former suitor. Dressed again as a British woman in search of the healing springs, she found herself in none other than the office of her old beau Ambrose Burnside. Burnside was now the head of the Union department of Ohio. He was fiercely prosecuting everyone he suspected of Southern sympathies, even old friends. Anyone convicted of aiding the Confederacy could be given the death penalty.

Whether she recognized Burnside immediately is unclear. It is also not clear whether Lottie needed a pass or was there to convince Burnside to release Ginnie and her mother, who were already in Burnside's custody for their own spying activities.

Regardless of Lottie's intent, she was going out on a limb to be in the presence of a Union general who was making a career of catching Southern sympathizers. She could not possibly have wanted Burnside to recognize her. In this aim, she failed. Burnside listened to her heart-wrenching story about her health and journey and her desperate pleas, whether for a pass or for the release of her mother and sister. Finally, he interrupted. "You've forgotten me," he said. "But I still remember with pleasure the hours I used to spend with you in Oxford."[2] Nervy as ever, Lottie denied ever having met the general. What was he talking about? She was just an old British woman trying to get to the springs.

Burnside was not having it, and Lottie finally gave up. Lottie joined Ginnie and Mrs. Moon in captivity. Here she waited to hear if Burnside would exact revenge for his broken heart of thirteen years earlier. Apparently he did not, as there are no records of her conviction. As the war came to an end, so did Lottie's espionage activities. Lottie and her husband moved to New York and lived happily among their former enemies, the Yankees. The war long over, Lottie put her talents to further use as a novelist and a journalist, even traveling to European capitals to cover the Franco-Prussian War.

5

Ginnie Moon: From Spy to Philanthropist

Like her sister Lottie, Ginnie Moon was a shameless flirt and bold spy who used her acting skills to smuggle messages and other items under Union officers' noses. Though she was fifteen years younger than Lottie, Ginnie had a similar temperament and career in espionage. She was also just as brash: though she never left anyone at the altar that historians know of, it's said that Ginnie Moon was at one point engaged to sixteen different Confederate soldiers, with the excuse that the engagements brought the young men joy as they risked their lives. "If they'd died in battle, they'd have died happy, wouldn't they?" she once said unapologetically. "And if they lived, I don't [care]!"[1]

At the beginning of the Civil War, Ginnie Moon had been kicked out of college. Surrounded by feverish Northern patriotism, she had announced to the principal her wish to leave. When he refused to allow this, Ginnie responded by going outside, taking her pistol, and shooting out every single star in the flag. In this way she won her freedom and prepared to join her mother in Tennessee. While she was waiting, Ginnie stayed with Lottie and Jim Clark. Here, Ginnie received a crash course in the art of spying for the Confederacy. Since she had succeeded in outdoing her sister in gathering fiancés, she was apparently going to try for the same victory when it came to spying.

Eventually, teenage Ginnie made it back to Memphis, where she and her mother tended soldiers in hospitals. Ginnie found this extremely boring. That summer, she watched as Memphis was invaded by federal troops. There were stories that she took information and supplies to the Confederate troops, was arrested, and then charmed her way out—but these stories were never confirmed.

An Ill-Fated Return to Memphis

In February 1863, Ginnie learned that the Knights of the Golden Circle needed a courier to take information from Mississippi up to Ohio. Naturally, Ginnie volunteered and convinced her mother to join her, insisting that they would not be suspected, as they had the perfect reason for a trip to Ohio: a family visit. Sure enough, they made it safely to Ohio and delivered the message.

Coming back was more difficult. At that time, Lottie's old beau Ambrose Burnside was heading the Union department in Ohio, making it his business to sniff out Confederate spies. Lottie and her husband were already under investigation. Around the time that Ginnie and her mother were preparing to return to Memphis, an undercover investigator was sent to the Clark residence. He was a charming young man who convinced the Clarks to let him in. In the Clark home, everyone welcomed him, but the agent found nothing—although he did note that the Clarks seemed to work at making quilts morning, noon, and night.

This sensational cover belongs to an 1861 book promising an "authentic history" of the Knights of the Golden Circle, a secretive Confederate society, allegedly by a "member of the order" itself.

Ginnie and her mother asked their new friend to help them get travelers' passes so they could head back to Memphis. The agent agreed, but he also sent a secret order to the boat captain not to depart until specific orders were received. Ginnie boarded the ship to cross the river looking like any other traveler. Kept secret from anyone else, however, she had a message wrapped in silk and tucked into her shirt. Her bags were also mysteriously heavy, and her skirt drooped.

The hour for departure came and went—and yet the boat remained docked. Ginnie and her mother sat patiently in their stateroom, quite sure they were on their way to complete their mission. But when Ginnie peeked outside of the stateroom, she later wrote, she "saw a Yankee officer coming through the cabin, looking at the numbers on the doors."[2] Upon finding Ginnie's cabin, he asked to come into her stateroom. When she agreed, he surprised her by locking the door behind him. He said he was Captain Harrison Rose and that he was with the Cincinnati Custom House. He had orders to search Ginnie and to deliver her to the provost marshal. He had a note with him that ordered her arrest, calling her a dangerous rebel employed by the Confederate government who had contraband goods and mail for the rebels.

Instead of surrendering, Ginnie reacted with scorn and disbelief. The officer moved to search her, but she stood her ground and all but shouted her indignation. It was almost unthinkable that a male officer would search a female suspect, but Captain Rose was unmoved. Calmly, Ginnie pulled a Colt revolver from the folds of her skirt and pointed it at the captain. "If you make a move to touch me, I'll kill you, so help me God," she told him.[3]

A politician from Mississippi who had served in both houses of Congress, Jefferson Davis was appointed president of the Confederate States of America in January 1861 and was inaugurated on February 18 of that year.

This, at last, was too much for the captain. When Ginnie invoked the name of her old friend Ambrose Burnside, Captain Rose agreed to have her searched elsewhere. He left the room momentarily. Swiftly, Ginnie locked the door, pulled her rolled secret message from her bosom, dunked it in water, and swallowed it. When Rose returned, Ginnie had her hat on and was ready to go.

Pushing through the crowds on their way to find Burnside, Rose remarked dryly to Ginnie, "I suppose you feel like hurrahing for Jeff Davis." Jefferson Davis was the president of the Confederate States of America. Thrilled with her success at destroying the message, Ginnie

Supplies for the Wounded

Today, it is known that keeping wounds clean and minimizing the spread of bacteria is crucial for ensuring that people don't become sick, but at the time of the Civil War, doctors had a very limited understanding of how to prevent infection. They also had little understanding of or access to anesthetics. On the battlefield, surgeons would operate on numerous soldiers using the same knife, "cleaning" it off on their dirty aprons between surgeries. Soldiers in the North sometimes had access to drugs like opium and morphine to help with the pain, but the blockades set up by the Union meant that unless spies like Ginnie and her mother smuggled drugs to them, Southern soldiers had nothing to numb the pain except maybe a little whiskey. Under such conditions, a good surgeon was a fast surgeon. Many soldiers died after enduring surgery, from infection or gangrene.

This illustration depicts Pickett's Charge, which took place on July 3, 1863, and was the last major event of the Battle of Gettysburg. Wounded soldiers, in pain and in need of surgical care and supplies like morphine and similar medicines, can be seen on both sides of the battlefield.

later wrote, "I raised my hand over my head and said in a loud voice, 'Hurrah for Jeff Davis!'"[4]

Caught with Contraband

Unfortunately, they were caught because of the supplies they were carrying. When Ginnie and her mother's bags were searched, incriminating evidence was found. There were bolts of blue gingham fabric, but this was nothing; Ginnie insisted it was to make children's aprons. (Actually, it was to make shirts for Confederate soldiers.) Worse, there were about fifty letters to people in the South—and opium. When questioned, Ginnie shrugged and passed it off to her mother. "Oh my mother can eat that much in a month," she said. Mrs. Moon sat straight-faced, and the officers tried not to smile. In fact, Ginnie confided in them, "She might be under the influence right now."[5]

She might have gotten away with convincing the soldiers that her mother was an opium addict, if not for the additional supplies of opium, quinine, and morphine found sewn inside Ginnie's unusually heavy collection of quilts. These were substances the South desperately needed to treat sick and wounded soldiers—and highly incriminating evidence to be found on someone suspected of sympathizing with the South.

As if it weren't abundantly clear at this point that Ginnie Moon was working for the Confederate cause, another discovery sealed her fate. Her hoop skirt got caught in the door, and when a soldier helped her to brush it out of the way, he noticed that it was strangely heavy. A housekeeper was called into the office to search Ginnie. Sewn into her skirts were forty bottles of morphine and seven pounds of opium and camphor.

After this shocking discovery, Ginnie could not complete her journey. She and her mother were placed under arrest. Ginnie pressed for decent accommodations. (Prisons were not considered suitable for women.) When she learned that General Burnside was staying at the Burnet House, she insisted that she and her mother be brought there.

A Pleasant Imprisonment

At the hotel, Ginnie settled into a decidedly cheerful version of prison life. Almost immediately, Captain Rose asked her to dinner. Ginnie responded cheekily, "Well, you're my jailer. I have to put up with you!"[6] While they dined, Rose held up a telegram and teasingly asked if she would like to know what was inside. They were in a hotel dining room. Ginnie knew he wouldn't make a fuss in public, so she snatched the telegram out of his hand and opened it. Inside was a message from a general in Nashville, ordering that Ginnie be sent to him.

But in the morning, Ginnie demanded a meeting with Burnside. Although it had been thirteen years since her sister had left him at the altar, Burnside was kind to Ginnie. He assured her he would try her himself. This left Ginnie greatly uplifted, and she began enjoying her period of confinement. She sometimes teased the Yankee officers, accusing them of stealing her undergarments. "I had not the slightest idea that my stockings, petticoats or corsets could be construed as government prizes," she exclaimed.[7]

Soon, Ginnie was being invited down to the hotel lobby to visit with staff officers. The pretty eighteen-year-old was being entertained so well by the Union men that she raised eyebrows. She later wrote, "The Yankee women in

This marker, erected by the Tennessee Historical Commission, commemorates Ginnie Moon, who spent much of her life in Memphis, though she spent the last days of her life in New York City.

the parlor looked very indignant to see their officers being so polite to a [Southern] woman."[8]

She was even asked to a play by a young Northern officer. When she responded that leaving the hotel would mean breaking parole, he sought permission from General Burnside. Ginnie waited eagerly for word that permission had been granted, then promptly refused to go. "My brothers are in front of your bullets daily," she said. "I wouldn't be seen escorted by a Yankee!"[9]

The End of the Confederacy

Charges against Ginnie were eventually dropped, and she returned to her life as a Confederate supporter. Evidence of her espionage eventually reached as far as Philadelphia, Montreal, and Nashville, though she was never convicted of any crime.

In the middle of 1864, she tried to leave the United States to join her brother in France, where he was waiting out the war. Along with her brother's wife and two children, she made the trip as far as Newport News, Virginia, before being stopped by Union officers. They demanded the women take a Union oath. Ginnie's sister-in-law complied, but Ginnie snorted at the request and refused. She was held in custody for a period before being asked to take the oath again. Still, she refused. Exasperated, the officers released her into Confederate territory.

In Memphis, Ginnie lived out most of her days, an eccentric Confederate supporter even decades after the South lost the war. For years, she dressed in old-fashioned silks and hats and never married. In her seventies, she decided to become an actress and headed west, where she acted in bit parts alongside the likes of Douglas

Fairbanks, a world-famous actor of the silent-film era. Still later, she moved to Greenwich Village in New York City, where she chain-smoked, drank mint juleps, and told of her past exploits. She died a vibrant single woman in 1926, at the age of eighty-one.

6

Mary Surratt and the Assassination Plot

Mary Eugenia Surratt was a boardinghouse owner and Confederate sympathizer who paid the ultimate price for her activities during the Civil War. A landowner, widow, and mother of three, Surratt was the first woman ever to be executed by the United States government when she was hanged for treason on July 7, 1865. What did Surratt do that was so unforgivable? She was a known associate of John Wilkes Booth, and in May 1865, Surratt was tried for conspiring with Booth and others to assassinate President Abraham Lincoln.

Although she was found guilty of the crime in court and subsequently executed, historians still can't agree whether or not Surratt was actually involved in the plot to murder the president. Some argue that she was actually innocent, merely the victim of circumstantial evidence and the unlikely recipient of a shocked nation's outrage. Ultimately, Surratt was accused of conspiring with Confederates and running a safe house for Confederate sympathizers. For her crimes against the United States, she was killed.

Nine alleged conspirators in the Lincoln assassination are shown here, including Mary Surratt (*center*), her son John (*bottom right*), and John Wilkes Booth (*top left*). Four, including Mary Surratt, were executed.

The Boardinghouse

Born Mary Elizabeth Jenkins in Maryland in 1823, Surratt grew up on a farm. Her father died when she was just two years old. When she was twelve, Surratt was sent to a Catholic boarding school in Alexandria, Virginia. Five years later, at seventeen years of age, she married John Harrison Surratt, the son of a wealthy planter. The couple inherited land outside of Washington, but a fire destroyed their property in 1851. Still, they continued to be prosperous.

Two years later, they purchased 287 acres (116 hectares) of land, where they built a tavern, a post office, and a polling place. It was also where they raised their three children, Isaac, Anna, and John Jr. By 1854, the Surratts' tavern had grown to include lodging for local travelers and was later called Surratt Hotel. The tiny community that formed around their holdings was eventually known as Surrattsville.

In August 1862, Mary's husband died. And although he seemed like a successful businessman, he left her in debt. Unable to maintain the property herself, she decided to rent the tavern in Surrattsville to a former policeman named John Lloyd. Little did she know this man would turn on her in her greatest hour of need. Meanwhile, by 1864, she moved into another house that she owned, this one in Washington, DC, which she had converted into a boardinghouse.

Even though Maryland and Washington, where the Surratts lived, were both part of the Union during the Civil War, many of their neighbors supported the South. Two of Mary's sons actively showed their support. Her eldest son,

Isaac, joined the Confederate army, and her other son, John Jr., became a Confederate courier.

As a courier, John mingled with many fervent secessionists. One of them happened to be John Wilkes Booth, a young man from a well-known family who would become famous as Abraham Lincoln's assassin. But by the time Booth made his first visit to Surratt's boardinghouse, on New Year's Day in 1865, his plan was not to murder the president. Instead, he wanted to kidnap him. Booth had already discussed his plan with Mary's son John, John's friend Louis Weichmann (a boarder at Surratt's house), and a physician named Samuel Mudd.

Because he knew the area, John Surratt Jr. agreed to guide Booth and his proposed hostage across the Potomac

John Wilkes Booth

An actor and Confederate sympathizer, John Wilkes Booth is best known for assassinating Abraham Lincoln. He was born in 1838 to an acting family and soon became a popular actor who was highly praised by audiences. Booth was vocal in his support of secession at the start of the Civil War, and he opposed the efforts of abolitionists. He hated Lincoln deeply and conspired with some Confederate friends to murder him and other Union leaders: Booth would assassinate Lincoln, while his comrades would murder Vice President Andrew Johnson and Secretary of State William H. Seward. Only Booth was successful. On April 14, 1865, Booth shot Lincoln while the president and his wife were watching a play at Ford's Theatre in Washington, DC. Booth himself was fatally shot two weeks later while on the run.

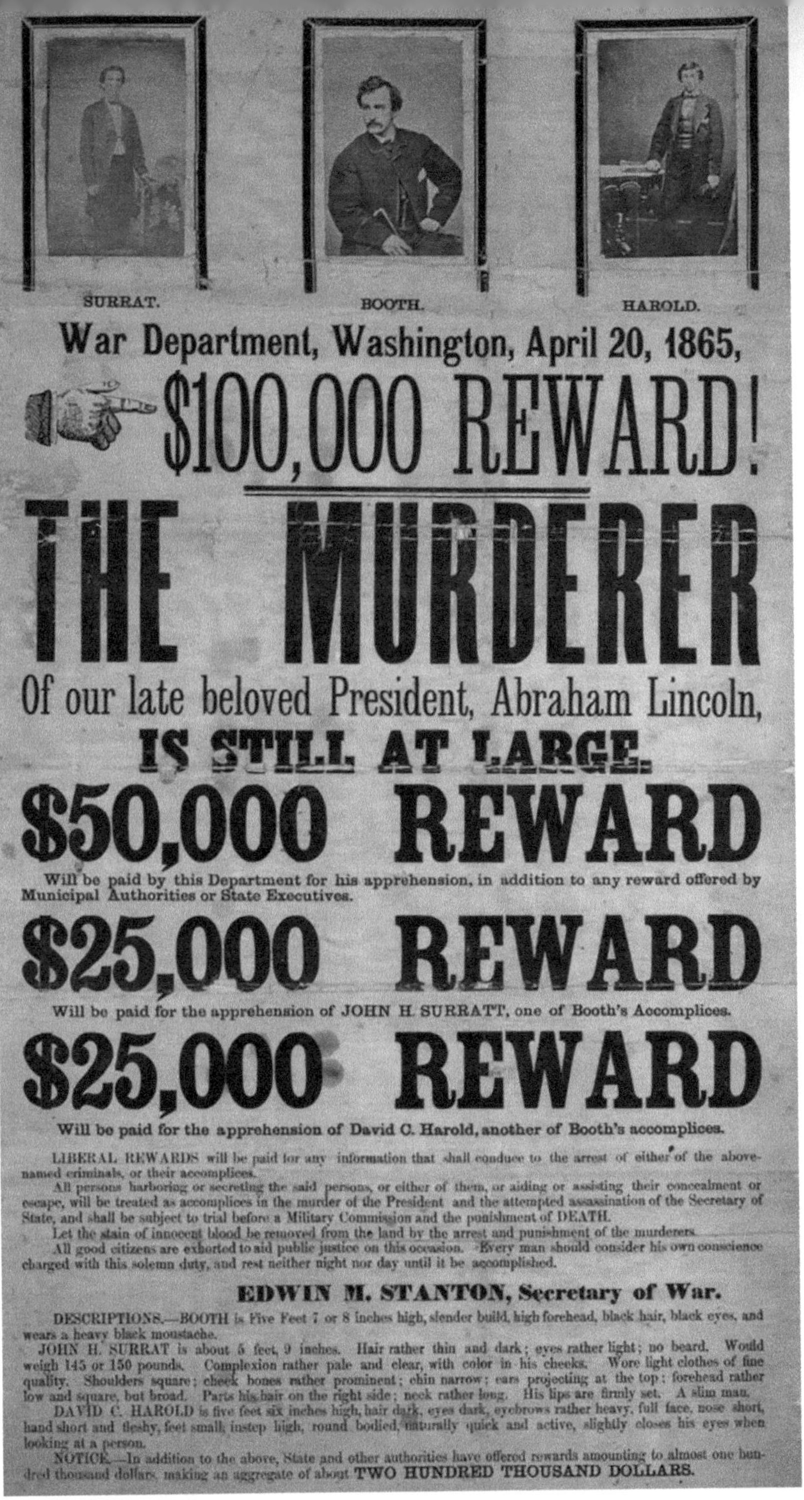

SURRAT. BOOTH. HAROLD.

War Department, Washington, April 20, 1865,

$100,000 REWARD!

THE MURDERER

Of our late beloved President, Abraham Lincoln,

IS STILL AT LARGE.

$50,000 REWARD

Will be paid by this Department for his apprehension, in addition to any reward offered by Municipal Authorities or State Executives.

$25,000 REWARD

Will be paid for the apprehension of JOHN H. SURRATT, one of Booth's Accomplices.

$25,000 REWARD

Will be paid for the apprehension of David C. Harold, another of Booth's accomplices.

LIBERAL REWARDS will be paid for any information that shall conduce to the arrest of either of the above-named criminals, or their accomplices.

All persons harboring or secreting the said persons, or either of them, or aiding or assisting their concealment or escape, will be treated as accomplices in the murder of the President and the attempted assassination of the Secretary of State, and shall be subject to trial before a Military Commission and the punishment of DEATH.

Let the stain of innocent blood be removed from the land by the arrest and punishment of the murderers.

All good citizens are exhorted to aid public justice on this occasion. Every man should consider his own conscience charged with this solemn duty, and rest neither night nor day until it be accomplished.

EDWIN M. STANTON, Secretary of War.

DESCRIPTIONS.—BOOTH is Five Feet 7 or 8 inches high, slender build, high forehead, black hair, black eyes, and wears a heavy black moustache.

JOHN H. SURRAT is about 5 feet, 9 inches. Hair rather thin and dark; eyes rather light; no beard. Would weigh 145 or 150 pounds. Complexion rather pale and clear, with color in his cheeks. Wore light clothes of fine quality. Shoulders square; cheek bones rather prominent; chin narrow; ears projecting at the top; forehead rather low and square, but broad. Parts his hair on the right side; neck rather long. His lips are firmly set. A slim man.

DAVID C. HAROLD is five feet six inches high, hair dark, eyes dark, eyebrows rather heavy, full face, nose short, hand short and fleshy, feet small, instep high, round bodied, naturally quick and active, slightly closes his eyes when looking at a person.

NOTICE.—In addition to the above, State and other authorities have offered rewards amounting to almost one hundred thousand dollars, making an aggregate of about TWO HUNDRED THOUSAND DOLLARS.

A newspaper ad offering a reward for the capture of John Wilkes Booth was published after Lincoln's death, before Booth was tracked down and subsequently shot and killed on April 26, 1865.

River. But two kidnapping attempts failed. By March 25, after many visits from Booth, John Jr. told his sister, Anna, that the actor was crazy. He asked her to tell Booth that he was not home.

The Assassination of Abraham Lincoln

On April 14, 1865, the day of the assassination, Mary Surratt traveled to Surrattsville with Louis Weichmann. There she found John Lloyd, the man who was renting and operating her old tavern. Lloyd was drunk, but this did not stop him from later testifying that Surratt had instructed him to have whiskey and "shooting irons," or guns, ready for whoever might show up later that evening. According to Lloyd, the guns had been left at the tavern several weeks earlier by John Jr. and two other conspirators in the plot, David Herold and George Atzerodt. Later that April night, after shooting the president, Booth showed up with David Herold at the tavern—as Surratt had anticipated, according to Lloyd.

Weichmann and Lloyd were both arrested, and after being kept in solitary confinement and threatened with being charged for Lincoln's death, they both agreed to testify against Mary Surratt. On the night of April 17, 1865, Surratt herself was arrested and taken from her Washington boardinghouse to the Old Capitol Prison. Within weeks, she was transferred to the Washington Arsenal Penitentiary, where the Lincoln assassination trial was later held.

The proceedings began less than one month later, on May 9. Weichmann testified that he had seen the accused men—John Wilkes Booth, Lewis Powell, George Atzerodt, and David Herold—meeting in Mary Surratt's boardinghouse. But Weichmann also testified that he had never heard Surratt express anti-Union sentiments. Friends and neighbors showed up in court to support this claim. Surratt was found guilty of conspiracy after John Lloyd became a key witness. As expected, he testified that Surratt had requested he have the guns ready for Booth and Herold as they made their escape on the night of the assassination.

On June 29, 1865, Mary Surratt, Lewis Powell, George Atzerodt, David Herold, Samuel Mudd, Michael O'Laughlin, Edman Spangler, and Samuel Arnold were found guilty of conspiring to assassinate the president. Surratt, Powell, Atzerodt, and Herold were sentenced to be hanged.

Although numerous appeals were made on Surratt's behalf, they were either ignored or never received by President Andrew Johnson. Awaiting a pardon, Surratt was hanged in Washington, DC, on July 7, 1865, along with the three others. She went to her death proclaiming her innocence.

Chronology

1860 Abraham Lincoln wins the presidential election.

South Carolina secedes from the United States.

1861 Six more states—Mississippi, Alabama, Florida, Georgia, Louisiana, and Texas—secede from the Union. With South Carolina, they form a provisional government, the Confederate States of America.

The Confederate Provisional Congress elects Jefferson Davis as its president.

Abraham Lincoln is inaugurated as the sixteenth president of the United States.

Confederate troops attack Fort Sumter, in Charleston, South Carolina, on April 12. The fort is surrendered the next day. This marks the official start of the Civil War.

President Lincoln calls for seventy-five thousand men to do a three-month stint in the army.

Four more states—Arkansas, North Carolina, Tennessee, and Virginia—secede and join the Confederacy.

President Lincoln calls for a blockade of Southern ports.

Richmond, Virginia, is declared the capital of the Confederacy.

The South wins the First Battle of Bull Run.

1862 Nashville, Tennessee, comes under Union occupation, debilitating the South.

Under Lee and Jackson, Confederate troops win the Second Battle of Bull Run.

Confederate troops are massacred in the Battle of Antietam, the bloodiest day in US history. Lee aborts his plan to invade the North.

Lincoln issues a preliminary Emancipation Proclamation, to take effect on January 1, 1863.

1863 The Emancipation Proclamation is formally issued by Lincoln.

The newly formed state of West Virginia is admitted into the Union.

The turning point in the war: Southern troops are defeated in the three-day Battle of Gettysburg.

Vicksburg, Mississippi, falls to Northern troops, giving complete control of the Mississippi River to the Union.

Lincoln delivers the Gettysburg Address.

1864 Ulysses S. Grant is named general in chief of the North.

Maryland abolishes slavery by a narrow margin.

Lincoln is reelected, despite his lack of popularity.

1865 Missouri abolishes slavery.

Congress passes the Thirteenth Amendment, abolishing slavery throughout the country. It goes to the states for ratification.

Wilmington, North Carolina, the last of the Confederate ports, falls to Union forces.

Lee officially surrenders to Grant at Appomattox Court House, Virginia, officially ending the war.

Lincoln is shot in Ford's Theatre on April 14. He dies the next morning.

Andrew Johnson is sworn in as president of the United States.

John Wilkes Booth, Lincoln's assassin, is shot and killed in Port Royal, Virginia, while trying to escape his pursuers.

Mary Surrat is hanged in Washington, DC, along with Booth conspirators Lewis Powell, George Atzerodt, and David Herold.

Chapter Notes

Chapter 1

Wild Rose Greenhow: Washington's High-Society Spy

1. Harnett T. Kane, *Spies for the Blue and the Gray* (Garden City, NY: Hanover House, 1954), p. 18.
2. Kenneth C. Davis, *Don't Know Much About the Civil War* (New York: William Morrow, 1996), p. 191.
3. Rose O'Neal Greenhow, *My Imprisonment and the First Year of Abolition Rule at Washington* (London, UK: Richard Bentley, 1863), pp. 23–24.
4. Greenhow, p. 29.
5. Greenhow, p. 56.
6. Greenhow, p. 25.
7. Greenhow, p. 290.

Chapter 2

Belle Boyd: The Siren of the Shenandoah

1. Belle Boyd, *Belle Boyd, in Camp and Prison* (Baton Rouge, LA: Louisiana State University Press, 1998), p. 49.
2. Boyd, p. 50.
3. Boyd, p. 82.
4. Boyd, p. 105.
5. Boyd, p. 106.
6. Boyd, p. 107.

7. Boyd, p. 110.
8. Boyd, p. 133.
9. Boyd, p. 145.
10. Boyd, p. 146.
11. Boyd, p. 149.

Chapter 3

Antonia Ford: Stuart's Southern Lady

1. Elizabeth D. Leonard, *All the Daring of the Soldier* (New York: Penguin Books, 1999), p. 95.
2. Harnett T. Kane, *Spies for the Blue and the Gray* (Garden City, NY: Hanover House, 1954), p. 171.
3. Leonard, p. 45.
4. Kane, p. 173.
5. Leonard, p. 49.
6. Leonard, p. 49.

Chapter 4

Charlotte Moon: The Costumed Messenger

1. Harnett T. Kane, *Spies for the Blue and the Gray* (Garden City, NY: Hanover House, 1954), p. 263.
2. Kane, p. 274.

Chapter 5

Ginnie Moon: From Spy to Philanthropist

1. Harnett T. Kane, *Spies for the Blue and the Gray* (Garden City, NY: Hanover House, 1954), p. 263.
2. Kane, p. 274.
3. Kane, p. 275.

4. Kane, p. 266.
5. Kane, p. 277.
6. Kane, p. 266.
7. Kane, p. 277.
8. Kane, p. 278.
9. Kane, p. 278.

Glossary

abolition The act of ending (abolishing) something, usually a practice or institution. In the context of American history, it usually refers to the fight to end slavery.

acquit To clear someone of criminal charges.

allegiance Loyalty to a specific person or cause.

camphor A natural crystal compound taken from the wood or bark of the camphor tree that was sometimes used as a topical painkiller during the time of the Civil War.

cipher A method of transforming text in order to conceal its meaning.

Confederacy The eleven Southern states that seceded from the United States in 1860 and 1861; the South. Members of the Confederacy were called Confederates.

espionage The act of spying.

lassitude A condition of weariness or fatigue.

morphine An addictive narcotic drug that is sometimes administered to relieve extreme pain. Morphine was available during the Civil War, though not widely.

myriad A great number.

notoriety Fame that comes from a person's perceived bad quality or actions.

opium A bitter, brownish, addictive narcotic drug that consists of the dried juice of the opium poppy. Opium was also available during the Civil War, though not widely.

quinine A natural crystal compound taken from the bark of the cinchona tree that was used for treating malaria during the time of the Civil War.

secede To withdraw from an organization.

treason An act of betrayal, especially to one's government.

typhoid fever A bacterial infection common in conditions where there is poor hygiene or sanitation that often proved fatal before the use of antibiotics.

Union Northern states loyal to the federal government headed by President Abraham Lincoln during the Civil War; the North.

Bibliography

Abbott, Karen. *Liar, Temptress, Soldier, Spy: Four Women Undercover in the Civil War.* New York: Harper, 2014.

Bakeless, Katharine, and John Bakeless. *Confederate Spy Stories.* Philadelphia: J. B. Lippincott Co., 1973.

Boyd, Belle. *Belle Boyd, in Camp and Prison.* Baton Rouge, LA: Louisiana State University Press, 1998.

Campbell, Helen Jones. *Confederate Courier.* New York: St. Martin's Press, 1964.

Chang, Ina. *A Separate Battle: Women and the Civil War.* New York: Puffin Books, 1996.

Davis, Kenneth C. *Don't Know Much About the Civil War.* New York: William Morrow, 1996.

Garrison, Webb. *Amazing Women of the Civil War.* Nashville: Rutledge Hill Press, 1999.

Greenhow, Rose O'Neal. *My Imprisonment and the First Year of Abolition Rule at Washington.* London, UK: Richard Bentley, 1863.

Halacy, Dan. *The Master Spy.* New York: McGraw-Hill, 1968.

Harriel, Shelby. *Behind the Rifle: Women Soldiers in Civil War Mississippi.* Jackson, MS: University Press of Mississippi, 2019.

Jones, Katharine M. *Heroines of Dixie: Confederate Women Tell Their Story of the War.* New York: Greenwood Publishing Group, 1955.

Kane, Harnett T. *Spies for the Blue and the Gray*. Garden City, NY: Hanover House, 1954.

Kinchen, Oscar A. *Women Who Spied for the Blue and the Gray*. Philadelphia: Dorrance & Company, 1972.

Leonard, Elizabeth D. *All the Daring of the Soldier: Women of the Civil War Armies*. New York: Penguin Books, 1999.

Mahoney, M. H. *Women in Espionage: A Biographical Dictionary*. Santa Barbara, CA: ABC-CLIO, 1993.

McCurry, Stephanie. *Women's War: Fighting and Surviving the American Civil War*. Boston: Belknap Press, 2019.

Pember, Phoebe Yates. *A Southern Woman's Story*. Jackson, TN: McCowat-Mercer Press, 1959.

Scarborough, Ruth. *Belle Boyd, Siren of the South*. Macon, GA: Mercer University Press, 1983.

Simpkins, Francis Butler, and James Welch Patoon. *The Women of the Confederacy*. Richmond, NY: Garrett and Massie, 1936.

Stern, Philip Van Doren. *Secret Missions of the Civil War: First-Hand Accounts by Men and Women Who Risked Their Lives in Underground Activities for the North and South*. New York: Bonanza Books, 1990.

Underwood, Rev. J. L. *Women of the Confederacy*. New York: Neale Publishing Company, 1906.

Wert, Jeffery D. *Mosby's Rangers*. New York: Simon & Schuster, 1990.

Further Reading

Books

Bozzone, Donna M. *Abraham Lincoln and John Wilkes Booth*. New York, NY: Enslow, 2019.

Cordell, M. R. *Courageous Women of the Civil War: Soldiers, Spies, Medics, and More*. Chicago, IL: Chicago Review Press, 2016.

Cummings, Judy Dodge. *The Civil War: The Struggle That Divided America*. White River Junction, VT: Nomad Press, 2017.

Monson, Marianne. *Women of the Blue and Gray: True Stories of Mothers, Medics, Soldiers, and Spies of the Civil War.* Salt Lake City, UT: Shadow Mountain Publishing, 2018.

Websites

American Battlefield Trust

www.battlefields.org

The American Battlefield Trust works to preserve battlefields around the country and has information and documents from a number of different battles and conflicts, including the Civil War.

American Civil War Museum

acwm.org

The American Civil War museum has one of the largest and most thorough collections of Civil War artifacts and documents in the country, much of which can be viewed through its website.

Civil War Women at Duke's Rubenstein Library

library.duke.edu/rubenstein/collections/digitized/civil-war-women

The Rubenstein Library at Duke University has a large collection of rare books and documents, much of which is digitized, including Rose O'Neal Greenhow's papers and the documents of other Civil War–era women.

National Women's History Museum

www.womenshistory.org

The website for the National Women's History Museum in Alexandria, Virginia, offers digitized exhibits, articles, and other resources about women throughout American history.

Index

F

G

H

J

K

L

M